Mom

FRIE

MW01672557

ST. JOHN NEPOMUCENE NEUMANN C.SS.R.

❀ WRITTEN ESPECIALLY FOR CHILDREN ❀

BY SISTER MARY PELAGIA LITKOWSKI, O.P.

For Renee La Bonte

With love,
Sr. M. Pelagia Litkowski O.P.

Copyright © 1987 by
Sister Mary Pelagia Litkowski
1st Printing – 1987
Revised, 2nd Printing – 1992
All rights reserved, including the right of reproduction in whole or part, in any form.

Published by

GROWTH UNLIMITED INC.

Dedicated to creating positive living concepts

Art Fettig, President
31 East Avenue S., Battle Creek, Michigan 49017

$3.95

Growth Unlimited books are available at quantity discounts with bulk purchase for educational, business or sales promotional use. For information, please contact Special Sales Dept., Growth Unlimited Inc., 31 East Ave. S., Battle Creek, MI 49017, (616) 965-2229 or 1-800-441-7676.

Manufactured in the United States of America

Design, Layout and Typesetting
by

GRAPHIC IMPRESSIONS

7261B Ohana Nui
Honolulu, HI 96818
(808) 422-6825

Library of Congress Catalog Number 87-80716
Litkowski, Sister Mary Pelagia, O.P.
Friend To All
St. John Nepomucene Neumann C.SS.R.
ISBN 0-916927-07-5

Acknowledgements

This life of St. John Neumann was based on Michael J. Curley's *Venerable John Neumann, C.SS.R., Fourth Bishop of Philadelphia*. N.Y., N.Y. Crusader Pr. ©1952. Before his passing, he read the first draft carefully and gave helpful suggestions and expressed the hope that it would be published.

Other sources of information were:

Autobiography of St. John Neumann, C.SS.R., Fourth Bishop of Philadelphia. Foreword by His Eminence, John Cardinal Krol, St. Paul Editions.

Flavius, C.SS.R., Brother. *The House on Logan Square: A Story of Blessed John Neumann*. Notre Dame, Ind. Dujarie Pr. ©1964.

Galvin, C.SS.R., James J. *Blessed John Neumann: Bishop of Philadelphia*. Baltimore, Helicon Pr. ©1964.

Langan, Tom; *Harvester of Souls: John Neumann*, Our Sunday Visitor, Inc. Noll Plaza, Huntington, IN 46750, ©1976.

Newsletter from National Shrine of St. John Neumann 1019 N. 5th St. Philadelphia, Pennsylvania 19123.

Sheehan, Elizabeth Odell *John Neumann, The Children's Bishop*. (Vision Books) Farrar, Straus & Giroux, N.Y. ©1965.

L'Osservatore Romano, June 23, 1977.

Hindman, Jane F. *An Ordinary Saint: John Neumann. N.Y.* Arena Letters, ©1977.

Thanks are due to the following:

Sister Jean Milhaupt, O.P., of the English Department of Aquinas College, Grand Rapids, Michigan, who read the first and second drafts and gave valuable suggestions.

Reverend Francis J. Litz, C.SS.R., former Vice-Postulator of St. John Neumann's Cause, who offered kind encouragement and prayers for the successful completion of this work.

Sister Carmelita Murphy, O.P., present Prioress General of Grand Rapids Dominicans and other former Prioresses General, Mother Mary Victor Flannery, O.P., Sister Mary Aquinas Weber, O.P., Sister Marjorie Vangsness, O.P., and Sister Teresa Houlihan, O.P., who gave permissions and kind encouragement.

Many of my Sisters and friends who listened patiently and gave encouragement and suggestions and offered prayers for the success of this work.

Sister Mary Pelagia Litkowski, O.P.

Foreword

We sincerely commend the writer of: *Friend To All* for her ardent zeal in giving wider play to the inspiration to be derived from the enriching example of one of our own U.S. saints: St. John Neumann, C.SS.R. To be especially commended is the easy readability of this biography with such a rich sprinkling of attractive anecdotes found in the saint's enthusiastic ardor for close imitation of Christ in his personal life and in the spread of Christ's church. To be especially noted is the Biblical quotation at the beginning of each chapter.

It is a very timely publication marking the 175th anniversary of John Neumann's birth and the 150th anniversary of his ordination to the priesthood. The author has devoted much time and study to this project. It should have a special appeal to younger readers, serving as a spiritual uplift in their courageous struggle to triumph over similar odds as did John Neumann in his diversified career. May this concise biography encourage all, especially our youth, to be satisfied only with the best in our human condition.

Rev. Francis J. Litz, C.SS.R.
Vice-postulator of cause of St. John Neumann
St. Mary's Church
Annapolis, Maryland

Dedication

For Sister Marie Vianney Giordano, O.P.,
who first introduced me to
St. John Neumann, C.SS.R.

The pictures in this book were reproduced by Sean McPharlan from pictures of the beautiful stained glass window scenes from Neumann's life which were published in the Shrine Newsletter.

Additional copies of this book are available from:

Growth Unlimited
31 East Avenue South
Battle Creek, Michigan 49017
(616) 965-2229 or 1-800-441-7676

IMPRIMATUR

Robert J. Rose
Bishop of Gaylord, Michigan
February 11, 1987

The imprimatur is an official declaration that a book or pamphlet is free of doctrinal or moral error. It does not imply that the one granting the imprimatur agrees with the contents, opinions or statements expressed.

1

Curious Child

"God made the two great lights, the greater one to govern the day and the lesser one to govern the night, and He made the stars."

Genesis 1:16

It was long past bedtime, the hour when all should be quiet in the Neumann (pronounced Noy-man) household.

"What's that loud talking?" asked Mother Neumann, hurrying up the stairs to learn what was happening. Sounds of a boyish voice came from John's room. They stopped when Mother appeared in the doorway. "John," she asked. "Why aren't you asleep? It's long past your bedtime."

"I was just wondering, Mother," John answered, "why doesn't the moon fall from the sky? What makes it stay up there? What keeps the sun and stars from crashing down to earth?"

"Never mind the sun, moon and stars now, John," retorted his practical mother. "Let God take care of His world. Get to sleep now or you won't wake up in time for Mass tomorrow."

It was John's turn to accompany his mother for Mass the next day. If he were not ready to join her, he would miss the "penny" she gave as a reward for coming with her.

Not many of John's companions came to Mass, Rosary, or Stations of the Cross as often as John did.

"Why don't you come to Church with me like John does with his mother?" asked one of the mothers of her son one day.

"If you gave me a penny every time I went, like John's mother does, I'd go, too," was her enterprising son's answer.

In Prachatitz, Bohemia, where John was born on March 28, 1811, of Philip and Agnes Neumann, children receive the Sacraments at an early age. John was baptized on the very day he was born. He made his first Confession at six and was confirmed at eight. He received his First Holy Communion at nine. It was then that little John Neumann began to know Jesus. His journey to holiness had begun.

"Our mother daily heard Mass, to which she took one of us."

2

Industrious Learner

"Receive my instruction in preference to silver, and knowledge rather than choice gold. For Wisdom is better than corals, and no choice possessions can compare with her."

Proverbs 8:10, 11

Even before he started his journey to holiness, John was busily travelling the path to learning. School began for him when he was seven years old. He had attended school for some time when his five year old sister, Joan, began to envy him.

"Please, will you take me to school with you?" she begged one day. "Please, Johnny?"

"Promise to be good?" said John, who knew what a little mischief Joan was. She promised. Off to school they went together.

On the way home that day, John scolded her roundly.

"I'll never take you to school again, Joan! How could you do that to me?"

At home, when Mother asked how Joan liked school, he complained before she could answer, "She liked it all right. She got all the attention, talking out loud and acting up. The kids thought she was so funny, they kept laughing at her instead of listening to the teacher. I'll never take her to school again."

Attention to his teachers and love of reading were two of John's strong points. He often took his books to the table in order to read while eating his meals.

"I don't believe he's really reading," his sister Cathy would say.

"He turns the pages too fast."

"Let's leave our little 'book worm' alone," was Mother's defense. "Some day he'll prove to us how much he's been reading."

John served Mass almost every day and had an altar at home at which he practiced Mass. But he did not think it possible for him to try so great a calling as the priesthood. Those who knew him, however, thought otherwise. Once when the family was beginning the Grace before meals, he made the Sign of the Cross the way a priest would make it when blessing the people.

"Look!" said an old servant of the family. "Johnny's going to be a priest!"

"How honored we would be if God should so favor our family!" exclaimed Mother Neumann. She sincerely wished that her little John would some day become one of His anointed ones. She often reminded him of the incident. This made a lasting impression on him.

"Whether he becomes a priest or not," observed his father, "one thing is for sure. He is doing well in school and when he finishes grammar school here in Prachatitz, we will send him to Budweis. There he can attend high school and college to prepare himself for a profession."

"Oh, thank you, Father, thank you!" exclaimed John excitedly. "I will study hard! I promise!"

"Well, at least, he won't become a barber, like he told the teacher once. He wouldn't have to go to Budweis to become a barber," teased his sister Cathy.

"I just said that because the teacher didn't give me time to think," said John. "I never intended to be a barber."

It was not long before, on November 1, 1823, John was on his way to Budweis. He and some twenty boys had to walk fifteen and one-half miles. The path to higher learning was about to begin for this future friend of God's people.

3

Diligent College Student

"Get the truth and sell it not — wisdom, instruction and understanding."

Proverbs 23:23

In Budweis, lodging for college students was hard to find. John's father made arrangements for him to stay with Mr. Eberle, a friend of the family. In order to cut down on his expenses, John agreed to room with three other boys. He soon found that this was a mistake.

His roommates cared little for study and much of their time was spent in noisy fun and games. Besides this, they had an aged, easygoing teacher who was overly fond of drink and he demanded very little from them.

"Please, fellers, stop the racket!" John would complain. "I can't think!"

"Aw, come on, Neumann!" his pals would taunt. "You know more than Tipsy's trying to teach us. You can join in the fun and still pass his exams!"

John felt that he was wasting his parent's money. He was not advancing in knowledge. He feared, too, that he was even forgetting what he had learned in Prachatitz.

Not long after this, a very strict professor replaced the easygoing one. He did his best to help his students make up for lost time. But they did not like the memory work he forced on them.

In his fourth year at Budweis, John went to live with a Mrs. Rudlof. She had a son who disturbed John's studying as much as his former companions had done.

"Send John to me!" scolded John's father, when he saw the report card he had brought home.

John came, looking sad and ashamed. "What does this mean, John?" asked his disappointed father. "I thought you wanted to go on to higher studies. Those marks are not what you are capable of earning! I think you better follow in your father's footsteps. You better become a stocking knitter after all."

"Maybe I should, Father," said John sadly. "That was the best I could do this time." He made no excuses for himself, nor did he complain about anyone who was to blame.

Mother Neumann and Veronica listened to this conversation with dismay.

"Why don't you give him another chance?" begged Mother Neumann. "You see how sad he looks. He does not want to knit stockings."

"Perhaps you are right," was Philip's answer. "We will send him to the professor who is visiting our pastor, for further testing. If he thinks our John is capable, we will send him back to school."

The professor did think John capable, and Mother Neumann and Veronica talked him into going back to school. He was happy once more.

This time John rented a private room, where there was no one to distract him from his studies. His marks improved and he made real progress. But his days were not all work and no play. The young people of his day had their dances and other social events. Even though John did not dance, he did join his companions in these events. He not only joined them but contributed towards their entertainment by playing his guitar. However, he was not in the habit of drawing attention to himself. On one occasion, so that no one would notice that he could not dance, he went to the refreshment room. There he helped to serve drinks.

To the girls, he was always polite and respectful. On another occasion, one of his friends put this question to him: "John, how do you feel about these lovely girls? Aren't they a real temptation to you?"

"Lovely they are, yes," was John's answer. "But to me they are like a beautifully bound book which I have not learned to read."

John loved his family dearly and often wrote home while away at school. Sometimes he drew pictures and sent them home for his little brother Wenceslaus.

In 1829 John finished his gymnasium course in Budweis and spent the next two years in the Budweis Institute of Philosophy under the Cistercian Monks of Hohenfurt. These teachers were very strict but very fair. John enjoyed his studies more than ever, especially astronomy and botany. He loved to go out late at night to study God's beautiful heavens, with his telescope to help him. He marvelled at the wonders of creation. The more he studied, the closer he drew to God. John also owned a microscope. With this, he studied plant and animal life. With some of his fellow students he formed a science club. During their meetings they shared with one another what they had learned.

John's school mates loved to visit him. They enjoyed looking into his microscope and playing his guitar. He always served their favorite snacks before sending them away.

It was in 1831, that John, at the age of twenty, graduated from the Institute of Philosophy. His marks were good, but he did not care to show them off.

It was time now to decide what his vocation would be.

"How can I be a priest, Mother?" asked John, when his mother asked if he were still thinking about becoming one. "I don't know any important people who would recommend me, and the Seminary won't take me without references. Besides, Father wants me to become a doctor."

Mother Neumann knew that John really wanted to be a priest. She urged him to try to enter the Seminary. This he did and was accepted. No matter how many people tried to talk him out of it, he was determined to become a priest. Now that his decision was made, he prepared to set out on the road to the priesthood.

4

Faithful Seminarian

"I will choose a faithful priest who shall do what I have in heart and mind."

I Samuel 2:35

It did not take John long to carry out his decision. On November 18, 1831, he entered the Seminary in Budweis. The Seminary was not large enough for all the seminarians. John, again, had to board with a friend, the widow, Mrs. Nowak. There were inconveniences and distractions, but John enjoyed the time spent in the Seminary. He advanced both in his studies and in his union with God. He had two close friends who were of much help to him, Karl Krbecek and Adalbert Schmidt. John did so well during his first year that he received the tonsure and took minor orders, the first steps toward the priesthood.

During the first two years in the Seminary, John had a teacher who made the seminarians memorize too much. He did not like this, but did his work just the same and received the highest marks possible in his studies. His behavior, too, was almost perfect. He overcame his dislike for memorizing and learned much of the New Testament by heart. He read the Scriptures daily. It was at this time, too, that he read missionary accounts of the work with the Indians in America. These stories fired him with zeal and he began to wish to imitate St. Paul who had done so much for the children of God, even though he was small, like John, and had poor health. John and his seminarian friends secretly made up their minds to become missionaries to America, after leaving the Seminary. And so, John began to do all he could to prepare himself for the rugged life he would have to live as a missionary in America. He studied harder than ever and began to learn English, Spanish, French and Italian, as well as German and Bohemian, so that he might be able to serve more people. English was not taught in the Seminary at Budweis. Therefore, John asked his bishop to permit him to go to the Seminary connected with the University of Prague, where he could study French and English. His bishop permitted him to enter that Seminary in September, 1833. There he also studied dogmatic and moral theology.

During the school year which began in 1834, new regulations from the government caused John Neumann much hardship. The seminarians were allowed to go for walks four hours a week. No visitors were permitted in the Prague seminary. Besides these regulations, there were rules forbidding the seminarians to take French courses. English was not taught. John had come to Prague purposely to get these two languages. Now he found that he would have to study them privately. At the end of the year he took the French examinations and passed. All his marks were very good. He worked so hard that he welcomed the Easter and summer vacations.

It was during the school year which began in 1834 that John started to write his diary. This account of his daily life gives us a description of his soul and spiritual life, rather than an account of daily happenings. It shows his perseverance in struggling against temptations, his faith and trust in God, his devotion to the Mother of God and the saints, and his determination to do the will of God. It is the picture of a soul that knew its own weaknesses, but was resolved to become a saint. Even the smallest faults seemed big to him and filled him with contrition. In his diary, such prayers as the following, show that he talked to God about his faults, begged for forgiveness and promised to do better:

> "Why this fear, as if there were no God?"

> "I still look more for the esteem of men than for Your Honor, O God of mine, but I promise to be more watchful in the future."

> "I must, henceforth, labor for the salvation of others."

> "Give me the grace which will aid me to obtain the perfection which You desire."

> "Give light to my eyes, O Jesus, that I may more clearly see the way to perfection."

> "Mother Mary, I am a sinner, but wish to perfect myself!"

That he had a loving concern for the people of God is shown in the following prayer:

> "Give me an ever increasing love for Your redeemed ones, that I may labor at their salvation in wisdom, patience and holiness. Grant that not one of those whom You have confided to me may be lost through my fault. Teach me how to live, and if need be, to die, for my people, that they may all be saved, that they may all love and praise You in eternity, that they may love Your dear Mother."

John did well in his studies during his fourth year at the University of Prague. However, he did especially well in catechetics. God was preparing him for the days to come, when he would be spiritual father to His people in the Family of God.

5

Priesthood and Missionary Aspirant

"The Spirit of the Lord is upon me... He has sent me to bring glad tidings to the poor..."

Luke 4:18

As the time for ordination drew near, John began to wonder about his future as a priest. The Diocese of Budweis had many priests and there was not much for a newly ordained priest to do. One day he was called into his Bishop's office.

"John," announced the Bishop, "we have received word that there is an opening in one of the secretaryships of the office of the government. Since we have more priests in our Diocese than there is work for them to do, we would like to offer you this opportunity."

"Thank you, Bishop, for this offer," was John's reply. "I do appreciate your confidence. But I really feel called by God to go out into the world to work directly for His people, for the good of their souls."

After this, John began to wonder if he would have a better chance of becoming a missionary and going to America if he joined some religious order. The president of the Seminary suggested that he join the Jesuits, but he did not think that he was suited for that great Order. In fact, he did not think that he was good enough to become a priest.

Before the school year was over, Bishop Ernst Rudzicka of Budweis, who was to ordain the seminarians, became ill. It began to look as if John's ordination would have to be postponed. In the meantime, his secret became known. One of his friends had told the president of the Seminary of his missionary ambitions. Fr. Dichtl, the one in charge of sending priests to America, began to make plans for him. Bishop Francis Patrick Kenrick of Philadelphia was asking for two German priests and Fr. Dichtl hoped to send John to him. What a disappointment John would have to face! He had planned on saying his First Mass in the presence of his family. He had hoped to give them all his priestly blessing. This was not to be.

John finished his studies in Prague and passed his examination in Budweis. Then he received the discouraging news that the Budweis seminarians would not be ordained at that time, because there were more priests in Budweis than there was work for them to do. It was in July, 1835, that the disappointed seminarian made his way to his home in Prachatitz. He wondered what was going to happen now. It would be hard to tell his parents that he was planning to be a missionary and that he might have to leave home before becoming a priest. He loved his parents dearly and did not want to hurt them. Fr. Dichtl, too, was slow in making arrangements for his missionary journey. This made him wonder if he was suited for missionary life, and if he was good enough to work for souls in a foreign land. He never stopped asking God for help and continued to put faith and trust in Him.

Finally, the day came when John had the courage to tell his family about his plan to be a missionary to America. They were stunned with surprise.

"Well, John," said his father, "This is not what I was hoping you would do, but if that is what you feel sure God wants you to do, I will not oppose His will."

Mother Neumann was utterly shocked. "Please, John," she begged, "think this over and pray about it. Before you take this serious step, be sure that it is your vocation."

They tried to hide their feelings. Their sadness, though, at the thought of his leaving home made it doubly hard for John.

Before John could leave, there were obstacles to overcome. He did not have a call from Bishop Kenrick and he did not have money to cover the expenses of the journey. No one seemed interested in helping him, but John was faithful to his resolution. Meanwhile, he made journeys on foot to many shrines in Bohemia and spent much time writing notes on the Old Testament and translating French spiritual works. He tried to live according to a schedule of prayer and work which he patterned after a rule of life he had found published in French.

At this time, some of the priests he knew began to help him collect money for the journey to America.

This time of waiting was not spent only in prayer and study. Whenever John could help his neighbor, he was not slow to do so. There was once a fire in a little village near Prachatitz which he helped to put out. It was a cold morning in December. Who would want to get out into the cold to carry buckets of water? John did it. Soon there was a bucket brigade helping to pour water on the flames. By the time enough help came, he was tired out. The people of the village were deeply grateful. They sent him a letter of thanks.

When John saw that it would be some time before ordination, he decided not to wait for ordination before leaving for America. He planned to go alone because there was not enough money for travelling expenses for more than one.

Because he wanted to spare his parents the pain of saying goodbye, he told his plans only to his sister Veronica, and left on February 8, 1836, without saying goodbye. His mother thought he was going to Budweis. He did go to Budweis, and from there, wrote a letter of farewell to his parents. In it he explained why he had left without saying anything. He thanked them for all they had done for him and told them he was sure that the sacrifice he was making for souls was the will of God. This sacrifice caused him much suffering because of his great love for his parents, and when he left them he felt that he would never see them again. Little did this lover of souls know what the future held in store for him. He was determined to serve God no matter what the cost would be. So, inspired by his trust in God, he pressed onward without so much as a backward glance.

6

Tireless Traveller

"...Go, therefore, and make disciples of all nations."
Matthew 28:19

"Man proposes and God disposes." John did not know that his journey to America was to be the starting point of much travelling in his life as a priest. A visit to Bishop Rudzicka in Budweis was the first step in his journey to America. He received the Bishop's blessing, but no papers, and hoped that everything would turn out for the best. He trusted in God for everything even though he was dressed poorly and had only forty dollars. His friend, Adalbert Schmidt, who had changed his mind about going to America, travelled with him by stagecoach for a short distance from Budweis. Sadly, John said goodbye to him and continued his travelling alone.

His first stop after leaving Budweis was at the Seminary in the city of Linz on the Danube River. There he met Bishop Gregory Ziegler, who encouraged him, gave him a letter of introduction, and promised to send help if he needed it.

John then travelled on to Munich, where he met an American missionary, Father John Martin Henni. Father Henni told him that Philadelphia did not need a German priest, but that German priests were needed in the Western part of the United States. This was disappointing news to John. He hardly knew what to do and called on God for help more than ever. A little ray of hope came to him when Professor Phillips of the University of Munich told him about the Bishop of Vincennes, Indiana, who was then in Europe looking for missionaries to take back with him to America. Father Henni gave John Bishop Bruté's Paris address. John decided to write to Bishop Bruté. Someone, too, gave John the address of a German hotel keeper in New York. This could help him if he ever reached New York.

John Neumann's next stop was at the Seminary at Strassburg. There he was told that the money promised to him for his travels had been given to other missionaries. How was he to get to America without money? The Superior of the Seminary, Canon Rass, said he would write to Bishop Dubois and ask him to take John into his Diocese.

After leaving Strassburg, John stopped at Nancy where he visited some Sisters from Bohemia. From Nancy he went on to Paris. On the way he met Father Schaefer, a missionary who was also going to the United States. John stayed in Paris more than a month waiting to hear from Bishop Bruté that he would be accepted, but John's letter must have been lost, for it never came. It was time for him to move on. He was running out of money. Knowing that German-speaking missionaries were needed there, he decided to sail for America, and thought he might even do missionary work among the Indians.

In spite of rain and muddy roads, John walked much of the way from Paris to Havre, where he arrived on April 7, 1836. At last, he was about to board the ship, Europa. He had to wait four days, but he never wasted any time. He prayed in Church, read and practiced English with a boy he had found in the neighborhood. He bought a straw mattress and pillow to use on the ship, which he boarded on April 11. He found that he had no privacy and that the passengers were not very friendly. However, he was so glad to be on his way that he was very happy. He wrote home telling his parents about his trip.

At last, Europa set sail on April 20. John had received word that there was little chance of his being accepted by Bishop Bruté. This, however, did not discourage him.

The voyage lasted for forty days. During this time, John spent much time reading, writing in his diary and praying that God would make him a good missionary. He also spent some time with a German and with a Mexican boy with whom he had made friends. Some of the other passengers made fun of him, but John was very patient. He had made up his mind to be like Christ.

One day, during the stormy voyage, John experienced a wonderful proof of God's loving care. He was standing alone in the prow of the ship. A voice within him seemed to tell him to move. As soon as he did, a mast fell on the place where he had been standing. Surely God was watching over him! More than ever he felt sure that his life was in the Hands of God and that he was headed in the right direction.

"What emotions were mine when I set foot on American soil."

7

Bohemian Immigrant

"...Go forth from the land of your kinsfolk and from your father's house to the land that I will show you."

Genesis 12:1

After forty days of sailing, the Europa came in sight of land at last and pulled into New York Harbor. The captain delayed the landing because of sick people aboard. John, therefore, begged to leave. He went in a rowboat to Staten Island. From there, he took the steamer Hercules to Manhattan. At last he was in New York! What did it matter if he had only one dollar and his clothes were worn? He was about to start his work for God in America!

He began to look for a Catholic Church in New York. When he could not find one, he stopped for the night at a Swiss innkeeper's tavern. This man gave him the address of a Catholic Church, Christ Church. From the pastor, John learned the address of Bishop Dubois and Father John Raffeiner, the Vicar-General of the New York Germans. Father Raffeiner gave John a warm welcome and told him that the Diocese of New York had accepted him three weeks before. This news had not reached him. They went to see Bishop Dubois, who was happy to receive John, as the Diocese of New York was badly in need of German priests. After hearing from John about his training in Europe, the Bishop was ready to ordain him without delay. John asked for a little time to prepare himself. How happy he was!

Without delay he went to Father Raffeiner's parish and there started teaching Religion to little children preparing for their First Holy Communion. He did this for two weeks. Then

Bishop Dubois called him for ordination. On June 19, 1836, he was ordained subdeacon. John was so thankful for this that he promised to say the Rosary every day all his life. On June 24, he was made a deacon. At last, on June 25, 1836, John Neumann was ordained a priest of God by Bishop Dubois. This great event took place in old St. Patrick's Cathedral. The Bishop was happy to have another priest to send to his German people. John sang his first Mass in St. Nicholas Church. The little children he had prepared for their First Holy Communion were there. They came after Mass to thank him and their parents gave him gifts. All this made him happy, but his joy was mixed with sadness. He missed his family and wished that they could have been present for his ordination. He offered this sacrifice to God for making him a priest at last, and permitting him to start working in the part of His vineyard that was the Diocese of New York. This Diocese was badly in need of churches for the many poor Irish and German immigrants who were pouring into New York at this time. There were not enough priests to take care of their needs. Father Neumann was given new clothes and expense money and appointed to the Buffalo District. He was eager to start work and left New York on June 28, 1836. Again he wrote in his diary: "I am in America, I am a priest, a missionary, and I have a flock!"

Before Father Neumann could start in Buffalo, however, Bishop Dubois told him to stop in Rochester to help take care of the German Catholics there. The people were so happy to have a German speaking priest that they wanted Father Neumann to stay with them. He began immediately to teach religion to the children, who had no school and were sadly neglected.

He prayed for these children and asked God to make him able to help them and their parents. The first time he administered the Sacrament of Baptism, he was so happy that he wrote in his diary, "If the child I baptized today dies in the grace of this Sacrament, then my journey to America has been repaid a million times, even though I do nothing for the rest of my life."

Father Neumann did not stay in Rochester because the Redemptorist, Father Prost, came to take over. Father Prost made a real impression on Father Neumann, who began to wish he could also become a Redemptorist, that is, a member of the religious Order, the Congregation of the Most Holy Redeemer.

Father travelled by canal boat to Buffalo and landed there on July 12. Father Pax, the pastor of the Catholic Church in Buffalo, welcomed him. Father Pax was not well and needed help badly. Besides the many Catholics in Buffalo to care for, there were people in settlements around it. Father was allowed to choose whether he would work in the city or in the missions around Buffalo. Father Pax advised him to work in the missions. This he decided to do, and went to work in the missions at North Bush, Williamsville, Cayuga Creek and Eden. North Bush had a church built of logs. Williamsville had a stone church. Cayuga Creek and Eden had wooden churches. These four churches were unfurnished. They were unfinished. Williamsville was made the headquarters and, because there was no rectory, Father Neumann went to live with a Catholic family by the name of Wirtz.

Father lost no time in getting to work. He collected enough money to finish building the church. Besides carrying on his priestly duties, he began to teach the little children in place of the teacher he had dismissed because of the teacher's misbehavior. It was seven months before he could replace the teacher. Father Neumann was good at teaching children. He told stories and gave holy pictures for lessons well learned. He taught the children to sing the praises of God in church. If they tried to get out of singing by complaining of sore throats, he coaxed them into singing by giving them candy. He always carried candy for the children.

After 1837 Father Neumann started a school in North Bush which he made his headquarters. In 1839 he started one in Lancaster. He persuaded his brother Wenceslaus, who had followed him to America, to help him in his teaching. With the added help he would now receive from Wenceslaus, Father Neumann felt that his missionary work could now really begin in earnest.

"St. John Neumann's love for children won him the title, Children's Bishop."

8

Zealous Missionary

"...Go into the whole world and proclaim the good news to all creation."

Mark 16:15

Father Neumann spent much of his time walking from house to house visiting sick parishioners, baptizing babies, helping the dying and bringing fallen away Catholics back to their faith. There were few roads and he walked, even through swamps, no matter what the weather, carrying his vestments and other necessities. On one of these occasions, he lost his way. It began to rain. After wandering from one path to another, he came at nightfall upon a little hut. In answer to his knock, a frightened little girl said, "Whoever you are, we cannot let you in. We do not let anyone in at night."

"Please let me in," Father begged. "I am a friend. I am a priest and I have lost my way."

Finally, the little girl opened the door. Father noticed that she was blind. When he entered, he saw a sad sight. The girl's father was lying on the ground and seemed to be ill. "I've been very ill," he told Father. "My wife and other children have died and my little girl and I are the only ones left. She is blind."

Father gave him some wine. This made him feel better and before Father left, the man made his confession. The story goes that when Father Neumann left, he had not gone far when he heard the girl calling to her father, "Daddy, Daddy! I can see the sky!" Truly, it was no accident that Father Neumann had lost his way!

Finally, Father Neumann's friends, out of sympathy, presented him with a horse. He had a hard time learning to ride it and more than once found himself thrown to the ground before he and his horse became friends. After much patient practice, he became a fairly good horseman.

He had many opportunities for practicing patience while working for God's people in America. Practice makes perfect and soon Father Neumann became known for his exemplary patience. When people came to him with complaints about fellow parishioners, he would say, "Let us pray about it. God will show us what to do." They would pray the rosary or some other prayers. Some people gave up their complaints after saying the prayers. Father Neumann practiced patience with regard to his own suffering as well. Even though his head was splitting, he never spoke of his pain unless someone asked him about his health.

At one time, a certain parishioner who was jealous because Father Neumann was staying with the Wirtz family, spread lies about him. Father proved his innocence by his quiet patience. However, he thought it best not to stay in Williamsville and moved in 1837 to North Bush where he was given a home, rent free, by a man named John Schmidt. This home was a mile and a half from the church. Father Neumann had to walk to church every morning.

During the time that Father Neumann lived in North Bush, the United States was suffering from a great depression. People were out of work and money was scarce. Father did not get much of his salary. He did receive corn and potatoes from the people. He did his own cooking until his brother, Wenceslaus, came in September, 1839. This was a great relief to him.

Father Neumann worked so hard that soon there were real improvements to be seen in his parishes. He continued the building of churches, starting of schools, and visiting the sick and the dying. He even helped with the building himself. At last he had a home of his own, which he had helped to build. It was built of logs and had two rooms. He was happy to live near the church where he could often visit Jesus in the Blessed Sacrament.

After Wenceslaus arrived, things became somewhat easier for Father Neumann. Wenceslaus helped with the teaching. He did the cooking and housework and helped with the building of churches, schools and rectories. Father hoped to make each of the missions ready for a separate pastor.

This good priest of God was never too busy for the children he loved. He made a schedule for himself to follow. He set aside the time from nine to eleven for teaching. The hour from eleven to twelve he also spent with the children. Again, in the afternoon, from two o'clock until four, he spent teaching. Certain parts of the Divine Office, the official prayer of priests, he prayed at special times throughout the day. He made resolutions to carry out practices which would make him holy. One of these, was making a visit to our Lord in the Blessed Sacrament every afternoon.

Father was determined not to be ruled by a love for money or things. At one time, he noticed how glad he was about the size of the Sunday collection. He made up for this feeling by giving away fifty cents to the altar boys. He resolved to do the same again if necessary. He promised God not to have anything more than he absolutely needed.

His long trips gave him a chance to notice the many kinds of flowers growing in the different sections of the country. He described them in his letters home and even collected samples which he sent home. One day when he was riding his horse past a pasture, he stopped to let his horse graze while he admired the flowers growing there. Father came upon a rare species of flower which intrigued him. He plucked it and, as he began to look for more, his hand felt a velvety caress and gentle tug. Turning again his attention to the flower he had admired so much, and which he hoped to add to his collection, he found, to his dismay, that it was gone! His horse had quietly ambled up to him and helped himself to the flower! It was too late. Disappointed, yet much amused, he watched the last petal disappear as the horse contentedly savored his tasty treasure.

So Father Neumann spent his days. Whenever God called him to serve the needs of His people in the classroom, in sickrooms, in field or in forest, there, Father Neumann could be found serving with all his heart and soul.

His first Mass prayer: "Dearest God, give me holiness."

9

Joyful Redemptorist

"I will proclaim Your Name to my brethren; in the midst of the assembly I will praise You... I will fulfill my vows before those who fear Him."

Psalms 22:23,26

In 1840, during the summer, Father Neumann became ill. The sickness lasted three months. More than ever, at this time, he thought he should join a religious order. This idea had been on his mind ever since his seminary days. He wanted to live according to a religious rule. The more he saw of the Redemptorist priests and their work, the more he wished to become one himself. He wrote to Father Prost, the Superior of the American Redemptorists at St. Philomena's, Pittsburgh, Pennsylvania. He received the habit of the Congregation on October 18, 1840, and began his period of training at St. Philomena's in Pittsburgh, Pennsylvania. There was no Redemptorist House of Formation in America. Therefore, he had to receive his training alone. He made meditations with the Fathers, said the Rosary, made visits to the Blessed Sacrament, and did his share of parish work in the Church of St. Philomena. He preached, taught Religion and administered the Sacraments.

Shortly after Father Neumann's arrival, his brother, Wenceslaus, came to Pittsburgh and became a Redemptorist lay brother. He was called Brother Wenceslaus. He was to spend more than fifty years helping the Fathers with their work.

Because there were not enough priests, Father Neumann could not live Community life in the Congregation as he had expected, but spent much of his time working alone. His place of work was changed often. In all his trials God blessed him with friends who helped him, and always he looked to the Mother of God for help and courage. After a short retreat, he pronounced his vows on January 16, 1842. He was the first Redemptorist to make profession in America. With peace and joy in his heart, he was now sure he had taken the right step and that he was ready for the missionary work of the Congregation.

As a full-fledged Redemptorist, Father Neumann started as an assistant priest at St. James parish in Baltimore. He did much to help the German immigrants there keep their faith. There was much to do because the German immigrants were increasing and there was a shortage of German speaking priests. The Bishops asked the Redemptorists to care for these immigrants in Maryland. Father Neumann travelled to the towns around Baltimore to give these people the spiritual help they needed.

After he had worked for some time among the German Catholics in Baltimore and the surrounding towns, Father Neumann was sent by his Superior to Pittsburgh where the new St. Philomena Church was being built. Bishop Michael O'Connor felt that Father Neumann would be a good pastor for the European immigrants in St. Philomena's parish. He could speak English, German, Bohemian, French, Spanish and Italian. Besides taking care of the souls of the people, Father Neumann faced the problem of raising money for the building of the church. He started a Church Building Society. Because the people were very poor, a contribution of only five cents a week was asked. This plan helped a great deal, but Father Neumann still had to borrow money. Often he did not know how he would be able to make his payments or pay his workers, but he always trusted God and God always helped him.

In 1845 there was a tragic fire in Pittsburgh. Father collected money from his parishioners to help the poor people who were suffering because of the fire.

Finally, the church of St. Philomena was completed and, in 1846, Father Neumann had a rectory built.

At the same time that he was seeing to the building needs in his parish, Father Neumann did much for the spiritual life of the people by starting religious societies. He was able to help his parishioners a great deal through the meetings, prayers and sermons. He also kept up three schools in the parish, which hundreds of children began to attend.

The priests worked not only in St. Philomena's parish, but travelled to neighboring parishes in surrounding towns where they took care of the spiritual needs of the people. Father Neumann worked tirelessly, sharing with his priests in the work of the parish. When they offered to take night sick calls, he sent them to bed, telling them they needed the sleep. He himself took very little sleep. Father Francis Seelos, one of the assistants, wondered how Father Neumann could keep on working. Much of his night was spent in prayer.

Bishop O'Connor was so pleased with Father Neumann's work that he wanted to make him his vicar-general, but Father Neumann did not want this high honor.

During his stay in Pittsburgh, Father Neumann had happy experiences and trying ones. One Sunday when he was celebrating Mass, a poor, fallen away Catholic stopped in at St. Philomena's beause he heard the singing and felt attracted to it. He took his place near the altar. The reverence with which Father Neumann offered the Mass brought home to him the truth that Christ had sacrificed His life for him on the cross. This affected him so forcefully that he wept. After Mass, he went to the sacristy and asked Father Neumann to hear his confession. Another prodigal son was reconciled to his Father.

At this time Catholics were suffering much from anti-Catholics who believed that Catholics were a danger to America. In Pittsburgh one of the churches was burned. At St. Philomena's one night, the school was set afire. However, the priests were warned and the fire was put out. Father believed this to be a proof of God's loving care and said it should make their trust in Him even greater. More and more, God blessed this new Redemptorist, more and more He prospered his work.

"First to join Redemptorist Fathers in America."

10

Humble Superior

"...There is no authority except from God... The ruler is God's servant to work for your good."

Romans 13:1, 4

Father Neumann worked so hard that soon he began to show signs of illness again. He began to have coughing spells and to spit blood. This caused his fellow priests to fear for his health. The higher Superior of the Redemptorists commanded him to see a doctor. The doctor ordered immediate care and rest.

Father was called back to Baltimore where he stayed during his convalescence. He took this change as coming from the hand of God and obeyed without delay. After his recovery he received a real surprise from the European Superior of the Redemptorists in America. This Superior appointed him Superior of Saint Alphonsus parish in Baltimore and General Superior of all the American Redemptorists. Father Neumann accepted this difficult assignment in the spirit of obedience in March, 1847.

The Redemptorists in America were happy to have Father Neumann in charge. They felt that he would help them keep their rule, promote unity and charity, and do much for the salvation of souls. His biographers tell us that he was most understanding, and that he always thought of others first.

It was during the summer of that year that a group of School Sisters of Notre Dame had come from Europe seeking a place for a Motherhouse for their Order. Father Neumann heard of the difficulties they were facing. He needed Sisters for his parish schools. He invited them to Baltimore where they bought a building that had formerly served as a Redemptorist Novitiate. These Sisters began teaching school in the Redemptorist parishes.

Two school Sisters of Notre Dame, whom Father took to visit the Redemptorist missions, told of an incident which showed Father's meekness. Once, while they were on a boat, Father Neumann was resting on a deck and fell asleep. Some boys took this chance to play a trick on him. They took chalk and marked all over the back of his coat. When he awoke and saw what happened, he just brushed off the coat saying that it would soon wash off. It was the same whenever anyone insulted him. He never let himself be disturbed by insults.

At about this time, Father Neumann also came to the rescue of another community of Sisters who were on the verge of disbanding because their Archbishop believed their efforts were failing. These were the Oblate Sisters of Providence of Baltimore, Maryland, a community of black Sisters. Father Neumann believed in these Sisters and their work. Besides giving them conferences himself and hearing confessions, he obtained permission from the Archbishop to send them one of his priests who would act as their chaplain. Thanks to his fatherly solicitude, these Sisters are a flourishing and zealous community in our country today. They are now an integrated community, though most of their members are black.

Father Neumann was especially interested in the education of children and often visited the schools. He sometimes took the place of a Sister who could not teach because of sickness. The children loved him and knew that he loved them. He carried candy and holy cards in his pockets for the little ones and was successful in winning their attention. He kept more than one child from being expelled and once taught a boy an hour each day until the boy changed for the better and surprised everyone by the progress he made in his lessons.

It was not easy to be responsible for the building of churches and schools when priests and money were lacking, but Father Neumann was encouraged when he saw how much good the Redemptorists were doing for the German Catholics in Virginia, Maryland, Pennsylvania, New Jersey, New York and the midwestern states. He continued to work conscientiously and tirelessly in spite of difficulties, until January, 1849, when Father Bernard Hafkenscheid was appointed to succeed him.

"All Sisters were befriended by him."

11

Citizen, Bishop, Lover of Souls

"We have passed from death to life, because we love the brothers... Let us love in deed and in truth."

John 3:14, 18

By the time Father Hafkenscheid took his place, Father Neumann was a real American. He had become a citizen on February 10, 1848. Now that he was no longer in charge of his Order in America, his work was easier, but Father Neumann did not intend to work any less for the people of God. Father Hafkenscheid appointed him as his consultor, and received much consolation and help from him. He helped Father Hafkenscheid with his work as Superior, did parish work, took charge of students, and directed many communities of Sisters in their religious life. He was glad to have some time for his own soul. He also did some writing. Among his writings were a bible history and two German catechisms which were used for a long time in German churches and schools.

It was not long before Father Neumann was given great responsibilities again. In 1851 he was made rector of St. Alphonsus Church in Baltimore. It was during that year that the Archbishop of Baltimore, Francis Patrick Kenrick, began going to confession to Father Neumann. Archbishop Kenrick had been Bishop of Philadelphia for many years. When he was made Archbishop of Baltimore, Philadelphia was without a bishop. The more he learned about Father Neumann, the more he began to think that he would make a good bishop for Philadelphia. This diocese needed a bishop who would be able to speak the German language. Father Neumann would be able to do this. He was also learned, pious, prudent and zealous. His name, along with two others, was recommended to the Holy Father. Father Neumann himself, was the last one to think he would ever be a bishop and when he heard of the possibility he could scarcely believe it. He begged his Superiors to prevent his selection and asked many Sisters to pray that it would not happen. However, such was not God's will. On February 1, 1852, Pope Pius IX appointed Father Neumann, Bishop of Philadelphia. When he learned what had happened, he spent a whole night in prayer. He became officially the Bishop of Philadelphia on Sunday, March 28, 1852, the day on which he was consecrated. He took as his motto: "Passion of Christ, strengthen me!" His parishioners were very proud of him. They would miss him, but they were happy for the people of Philadelphia. They gave him a farewell greeting which expressed the hope that he would someday be a saint in heaven. They also gave him a farewell gift of money.

Before Bishop Neumann left St. Alphonsus parish, he paid a farewell visit to the children in his three Redemptorist schools and told them always to be faithful Catholics.

This great change in his life was not an easy one. Bishop Neumann found it hard to leave the people of his parish and his fellow Redemptorist priests, but it was God's will. He prayed for the grace to accept it, and received that grace.

A group of priests met Bishop Neumann and welcomed him when he arrived in Philadelphia. The Catholics of the diocese would have been there, too, but they were advised not to come. Some of them approached one of the priests asking, "Why can't we welcome our new Bishop?"

"Because, my dear people," replied the priest, "your new Bishop does not like worldly honors. Why not show your gratitude for his appointment as bishop of your diocese by building a new school? This would be very much more pleasing to Bishop Neumann."

Nevertheless, the people did fill St. John's Pro-Cathedral when their Bishop was installed and he gave them a fatherly blessing.

There were many problems to solve in the diocese at this time. Many immigrants were coming from Europe. New churches were needed in order to teach the Catholic Faith to these children. More priests, brothers and sisters were needed. These, along with the regular duties of a bishop in caring for the spiritual and temporal welfare of a diocese, were the problems which Bishop Neumann faced. Knowing that it was God's will for him, he lost no time in getting to work. He began immediately to visit his parishes, to preach sermons, and to administer the Sacrament of Confirmation. His many problems caused him sufferings difficult for him to bear. In love of neighbor, he never wavered. In his journal he wrote the following prayer:

> "Speak to me, O my God, let me know Thy will, for behold I am ready to fulfill Thy every command. The difficult, the irksome, I will patiently endure for love of Thee."

He reminds us of Pope John XXIII, who visited even prisoners in jail; also, Pope John Paul II, who did the same. Once Bishop Neumann visited two prisoners who were in jail for committing murder. They were Catholics, but would not make their peace with God. After the Bishop's visit, they promised to do so, and when Bishop Neumann sent a priest to them they kept their promise before they were put to death on the gallows.

Again in his journal he wrote:

> "In my faint-heartedness, I indulged in wild dreams. To escape the terrible responsibility resting upon me, I sometimes thought of abandoning my flock, of fleeing to some distant solitude where I might lead a hidden, penitential life, or hire myself as a laborer in the fields. The fear of creating suspicion in the minds of the faithful and of affording the enemies of our holy religion occasion to blaspheme, alone prevented my carrying out this project."

Although he was not a great preacher, Bishop Neumann was so gentle, loving and sincere that he soon won the hearts of his spiritual children. In his letters he asked them to help him with their prayers and support.

All his life Bishop Neumann had realized the importance of religion in the education of children. Wherever he worked, he encouraged the establishment of Catholic schools. At the time he became bishop, he was determined to increase the number of schools and the number of children attending them. At a meeting held in the Bishop's home on May 5, 1852, a Central Board of Education was started for the diocese. This Board was to help in the school building program. It was the beginning of the unification of the diocesan-wide parochial school system of today. Besides giving financial help and directing the schools in a general way, it started a society called "Young Catholics Friends Society," which was to help in the education of poor Catholic children. More schools were built until most of the parishes had schools and, instead of a few hundred, thousands of Catholic children were attending parochial schools.

In spite of his many duties, one of Bishop Neumann's significant achievements was the writing of a German catechism for the German children of the diocese. This was approved by the First Plenary Council of Baltimore.

"Principally through his prodigious efforts a Catholic school system came into being."

12

Builder of Churches

"Then I explained to them how the favoring Hand of my God had rested upon me. They replied, 'Let us be up and building!' And they undertook the good work with vigor."

Nehemiah 2:18

Under his direction and encouragement many new churches were built. Since bishops were supposed to visit their parishes every two years, Bishop Neumann did his best to do so. Sometimes he even travelled on foot to reach some of his parishes. Once he walked many, many miles to confirm one boy. To him every child of God was important. During his visits he heard confessions, made sick calls, even said Mass in the homes of sick people who lived far from the church. He preached some sermons and administered the Sacrament of Confirmation. Often he visited his beloved children in the schools. Two little girls especially had reason to remember for many years afterwards, how they managed to get from him a proof of his love. The Holy Cross Sisters had sent them to the Bishop's residence on an errand. Bishop Neumann came upon them in the parlor admiring a beautiful statue of a child in a crib.

"Father, we like your crib with the pretty baby in it, so much! We wish we had one like it!" exclaimed one of the girls, when she saw the Bishop.

"Well, now, my little friend," said Bishop Neumann, when he saw how much they liked it, "I promise to give this one to the one who can carry it home."

"Honest?" cried the girls with wide-eyed surprise.

"Honest!" came the unexpected reply.

The statue weighed about twenty or twenty-five pounds. Taking the Bishop at his word, one of them, Margaret McSheffery, ran home and soon returned with a little wagon. What could Bishop Neumann do but keep his word? He also predicted this girl's entry into the convent and that she would become the Mother General of the Holy Cross Sisters. This prediction came true and she kept the statue all her life. It still stands in a place of honor in the Holy Cross Motherhouse, St. Mary's, Notre Dame, Indiana.

Surely Bishop John Neumann could be called anyone's friend. Nothing could keep him from his people. They saw how his heart was on fire with zeal for the good of their souls and they loved him for it.

The practice of having Forty Hours Devotion in honor of Jesus in the Blessed Sacrament regularly every year for so many years in our churches was promoted by Bishop Neumann. At that time, some of his priests were afraid that the enemies of the church would dishonor the Blessed Sacrament if this devotion were held often and it came to their attention. Something happened which made the Bishop feel sure he should not hesitate to carry out his plan.

One night as Bishop Neumann sat at his desk working, he fell asleep because he was exhausted from the day's work. The burning candle on the desk was still burning to its end when he awakened. To his surprise, the papers on the desk had been scorched, but they were not destroyed, and the writing on them was still intact. He thanked God for this. It seemed to him that God spoke to him, telling him not to be afraid that the Blessed Sacrament would be dishonored, because his plan for the Forty Hours Devotion would bring honor and glory to God. This devotion soon spread throughout the dioceses of the United States and did promote devotion to Jesus in the Blessed Sacrament.

13

Lover of Home

"Go home to your family and make it clear to them how much the Lord in His Mercy has done for you."

Mark 5:19

In 1854 Bishop Neumann had the joy of a trip to Europe. He was present in Rome for the proclamation of the Church's teaching on the Immaculate Conception of the Blessed Virgin Mary. He made his official visit to the Holy Father and then he visited his family in Prachatitz, Bohemia. He had never expected to see his family again and this visit was a great joy to him. He tried to come home quietly and simply, but in this he failed. His friends learned of his coming, and, in spite of cold and snow, came to welcome him. When he arrived in Prachatitz, the first place he visited was the church, where he greeted our Lord in the Blessed Sacrament. Then, in the midst of a joyful crowd of people, he walked home. His father took him up in his arms and happily embraced him. He spent one week with his family and friends in Prachatitz. It was a week they would never forget. He celebrated the Eucharist with them, preached sermons and attended parties they gave for him.

In order to avoid any more honors, Bishop Neumann left Prachatitz early one morning before anyone knew that he was leaving. A priest that was with him told how his eyes filled with tears when he looked at his home town for the last time. He would never forget God's goodness in granting him this happy visit with his loved ones.

"Death in the Master's service."

14

Faithful Friend to All

"He who is a friend is always a friend."

Proverbs 17:17

After visiting some of his fellow Redemptorists and other friends, Bishop Neumann sailed for America and arrived safely on March 28. When he reached Philadelphia, the people there were very much relieved as they had been worried about him because of the many terrible storms which had been raging on the Atlantic Ocean during that month.

Once again in America, Bishop Neumann went diligently back to work. Besides the schools and churches, he started an orphanage, a new Order of Sisters called the Third Order of St. Francis, and a seminary.

In a short biography it is not possible even to begin to tell everything Bishop Neumann did in his brief span of life. This good friend of God's people was only forty-eight years old when God called him home to Himself. On January 5, 1860, he went out on business as usual and was walking along one of the streets in Old Philadelphia when he fell to the ground. It was an attack of apoplexy. He was carried to one of the homes and while there, he breathed his last. The priest who had been called arrived too late, but he anointed the Bishop and prayed for his soul.

Bishop Neumann's death brought sadness to the hearts of all his people. They came by the thousands to view his body. The crowd at the funeral services was believed to be the largest there had ever been in Philadelphia. Men, women and children came, weeping at the loss of one they knew had been a **Friend To All**. They believed him to be holy. They knew how much he loved all God's people.

He was buried in St. Peter's Church. People began to visit his tomb and pray to him. Many favors were reported, proving that he was, in death as well as in life, a **Friend To All.** His life was written and published. The Church investigated his virtues and in December, 1921, Pope Benedict XV declared Bishop Neumann *Venerable*. This was the first step towards his canonization. The Church continued to investigate his life. People continued to pray to him, asking him to intercede for favors and then receiving them. Two more first class miracles were approved. A little girl was cured of peritonitis and a man who had suffered a fractured skull was cured. In October, 1963, a seven-year old boy who was suffering from cancer of the leg was taken to Bishop Neumann's Shrine. The following January found the boy cured of cancer after a relic of Blessed John Neumann had been applied to his leg. Doctors had pronounced him incurable and had predicted certain death. The Medical Board for the Sacred Congregation for the Causes of Saints declared that the cure could not be explained medically or scientifically. This was a first class miracle which was needed for Blessed John Neumann's canonization. Many other thanksgivings for the favors people were receiving continued to pour into the Blessed John Neumann Center in Philadelphia. Here Rev. Francis J. Litz was Vice-Postulator of the Cause of Bishop John Neumann. Finally on June 19, 1977, our Holy Father, Pope Paul VI, during a Mass held in St. Peter's Square, canonized Bishop John Neumann. In his homily, Pope Paul summarized St. John's life and showed how, in his priestly zeal, he laid down his life for the people of God in America, to serve whom he had been sent. He called St. John Neumann "an effective witness in his generation to God's love for His Church and the world," and "a true example for all of us" in regard to God's plan of love in our lives. He declared that the ceremony of this canonization was a "celebration of holiness for the Church, for the United States, for the world, of a renewal in love, love for God, love for neighbor."

"John Neumann envisions missionary vocation to save faith of immigrants to America."

Postlude

Not infrequently it happens that once a Blessed has been canonized, we hear little about him or her. Public prayers and devotions are no longer held and the holy one is practically forgotten. This has not been so with St. John Neumann. His devotees continue to make known his powerful intercession with God, to publish favors received and to conduct devotions in his honor. They continue to present to the people of God this model of Christlikeness which Pope Paul VI encourages all of us to imitate.

Today, the most outstanding center promoting devotion to St. John Neumann is the *National Shrine of St. John Neumann, CSSR,* at St. Peter the Apostle Church, Fifth Street and Girard Avenue, Philadelphia, Pennsylvania, 19123. Here special Shrine Services are held in his honor daily. Here one can learn of the life this holy man lived. Crowds of the people of God come to enrich their lives or to regain peace of soul.

An annual *Children's Day* is held in honor of this special lover of children with a view to increasing religious and priestly vocations. Many children come to take part in the procession and to receive the blessing.

Schools, Societies, Senior Citizen groups and Confraternities from throughout the world still conduct pilgrimages to the Shrine, where Masses and Novena Services are conducted for them daily.

A *Family Radio Rosary* over Station WIBF-FM 104 broadcasts a program daily at 1:00 P.M.; on Saturdays, at 9:00 P.M. with "Christian Hero Story", and on Sundays at 7:30 P.M. On First Saturdays, a Nuns' Holy Hour and Mass are scheduled at 10:00 A.M. and a prayer Vigil from 12:00 to 3:00 P.M.

There is also a daily telephone program called *Dial-A-Message*. An uplifting spiritual message (changed every day) can be received from anywhere in the country by calling (215) 627-6110. The sick, the lonely and shut-ins derive great consolation from this daily telephone program.

The Museum and Exhibit are open every day from 9:00 A.M. to 4:00 P.M.

Special Blessings of the sick are conducted.

The Shrine is headquarters for the *St. John Neumann Guild*. Members share in the prayers offered at the Shrine, in 70 Masses each year, and receive a *Newsletter* four times a year. This *Newsletter* brings them the latest news about favors received through St. John Neumann's intercession and activities held in his honor. Letters of thanksgiving continue to come. Truly, St. John Neumann still is and will continue to be **Friend To All.**

For other information on St. John Neumann contact:

The National Shrine of St. John Neumann
1019 North Fifth Street
Philadelphia, PA 19123
Phone: (215) 627-3080

"Pilgrims at the shrine kneel at his tomb asking for his intercession."

Prayer in Honor of St. John Neumann for the Welfare of the Catholic School System

God of ages, in Your kind providence, You watch and guide with loving care every age of our earthly existence and progress.

Saint John Neumann was an instrument in Your hands in bringing such rich blessings on our forefathers in this land which has chosen Your own Blessed Mother as its Patroness. Through their intercession look down with compassion on our present day needs. Grant especially renewed strength and healthy growth to our parochial school system and our secondary education endeavors. Grant that these schools may be financially sound. Grant that they may be instrumental in inspiring our energetic youth of today with the desire to dedicate their life's career to consecrated service in your vineyard as priests, religious and apostolic workers. Grant to Your American children a deep love and respect for St. John Neumann and confidence in him as our model and intercessor, one who was, in his day, the zealous promotor of the Catholic school system in its infant days. Take care of this vine, Protect what Your right hand has planted. This we ask through Christ, our Lord.

Amen

Prayer for Graces Through the Intercession of St. John Neumann

Merciful Father, You have given me all that I have in this world, even life itself. In all my daily needs, help me to remember the needs of others, too. Make me aware of the need to pray to You, not just for myself, but for the church, the Pope, for the clergy and for people who suffer any need. Make me selfless as St. John Neumann was. Throughout my life, give me the grace to direct my first thoughts to the service of You and of others. Make my prayer — "Your will be done" knowing that in Your mercy and love, Your will for me is my sanctification. I ask this, through Jesus Christ, our Lord.

Amen

Saint John Neumann, pray for us.

Biography

Sister M. Pelagia O.P. was born Florence Irene Litkowski in Saginaw, Michigan, where she was educated in high school by the Grand Rapids Dominican Sisters. She made Profession as a Dominican Sister at Marywood in Grand Rapids, Michigan in 1934 and taught in Catholic Elementary Parochial Schools in Michigan until 1961 when she received a Masters Degree in Librarianship from Western Michigan University in Kalamazoo, Michigan, and took up her second career as a librarian in several parochial schools in Michigan.

Presently she is librarian at St. Michael School in Fremont, Michigan.

Her life-long hobby has been writing plays, letters to editors and newspaper articles. The many blessings she has received through St. John Neumann's intercession have inspired her to write the biography of this great American Redemptorist saint. She resides at St. Michael Convent, 10250 N. Maple Island Rd., Fremont, Michigan, 49412.

Aftermath

From all over the United States, come letters to the *National Shrine of St. John Neumann* attesting to the power of his intercession with God.

Among these letters of thanksgiving are those coming from the following states:

From New York

A client of St. John Neumann, who had not been in church for twelve years, and who was suffering from an emotional crisis, heartbreak and loneliness, went to St. Patrick's Cathedral, lighted a candle at St. John Neumann's Shrine there and prayed. He himself was relieved, his sister's marriage was saved, a friend was cured of cancer and the daughter of another friend was admitted to a sanitorium, after they had lost all hope of admission.

A man from Elma, New York, was not expected to survive surgery for cancer of the stomach because of his heart condition. His wife pinned a relic of St. John Neumann to the back of his wrist watch. The surgery was successful. His heart became normal. The doctor declared this a miracle because medicine had not helped. After six months, the man was declared free of cancer cells and his heart was better than it had been in five years.

A doctor from Cebu, Philippines, recovered from liver cirrhosis and fluid accumulation of the abdomen after the intercession of St. John Neumann was sought during a pilgrimage made by his relatives to the Shrine in Philadelphia for his miraculous cure. His doctor attributed this to St. John Neumann's intercession.

A Novena was made to Mary and St. John Neumann for an 18 year-old boy who had terminal cancer, asking them to pray that, if he was not cured, God would give him the grace to suffer willingly and to accept His will. Hardly had the novena been started when the boy's pain left him. He began to eat and drink and the lump on his hip disappeared. The boy is living a normal life and his doctors don't know what to think of it.

From Pennsylvania

After receiving a copy of the St. John Neumann novena, a man who was looking for a job received it the day after completing the novena. He gives St. John Neumann credit for obtaining this favor for him.

After three weeks of medication with no resulting healing, a facial skin cancer was completely cleared up on the day after a St. John Neumann relic was used along with prayers for healing to St. John Neumann.

From Tennessee

A remarkable recovery from surgery was reported by a man who promised publication if he would be able to greet Father John Krimm and offer him assistance in finding his way around Knoxville after Father conducted a Triduum. It had not been believed that he would be able to accomplish this special duty because his surgery had been performed too near to the time of the Triduum.

From Maryland

Cure of a troublesome callous on his right foot and a remarkable improvement in health after surgery which resulted in inflammation, abscess, fistula and other ailments were reported, after the patient's prayerful visits to the Shrine.

From New Jersey

News has come of healing of psoriasis, infections, spinal meningitis, disappearance of cancer and emergency heart surgery. St. John Neumann's prayers have even obtained from God the possibility of motherhood for women who were told by doctors that pregnancy for them was impossible. Remarkable recoveries from injuries received in near fatal accidents have been reported.

From Ohio

A devotee of St. John Neumann reports that, after a severe back injury, he was in great pain and confined to bed, unable to walk. After making a novena to St. John Neumann, he found himself able to walk about the house and confident of a full recovery.

From New Mexico

After prayers to St. John Neumann, hearing completely returned in an ear in which doctors had declared it was impossible to restore hearing.

Highlights in the Life of St. John N. Neumann CSSR

1811 March 28, John Nepomucene Neumann, born in Prachatitz, Bohemia and baptized the same day.

1818 John received the Sacrament of Penance for the first time and started school in the same year.

1819 John received the Sacrament of Confirmation.

1820 John received his First Holy Communion.

1823 John entered secondary school (gymnasium) in Budweis.

1829 He finished secondary school and started to take advanced courses in Budweis.

1831 He graduated with honors and entered the diocesan seminary in Budweis.

1832 He received the first steps toward ordination: tonsure and minor orders.

1833 Oct. 8, he entered the archdiocesan seminary of Prague.

1834 He began his spiritual journal.

1835 He passed his ordination examinations in Budweis. Because no date was set for his ordination, he resolved to become a missionary to the United States.

1836 February 8, he left home on his way to America, and set sail on the ship Europa on April 20.

June 2, he left Staten Island, N.Y. and sailed to Manhattan.

June 19, he was ordained by Bishop Dubois of New York, as sub-deacon.

June 24, he was ordained a deacon, and ordained a priest on June 25.

June 26, he offered his First Mass at St. Nicholas Church.

June 28, he was sent to help Father Alexander Pax.

July 4, he stopped in Rochester to preach to the German immigrants and to hear confessions. Here he met Father Joseph Prost, a priest of the Redemptorist Order.

July 12, he arrived in Buffalo and chose to serve in the country districts outside Buffalo.

September, he moved to Williamsville where he completed the building of a church and started a school in which he himself taught.

1837 He moved to North Bush and started another church and school.

1839 John's brother Wenceslaus joined him at North Bush and began helping him in many ways.

1840 Fathers Pax and Prost assure him that it is God's will that he become a religious.

September 4, he requests admission into the Congregation of the Most Holy Redeemer (Redemptorists).

September 16, the Redemptorists accept him and send him to St. Philomena's in Pittsburgh, Pennsylvania.

October 18, he began his novitiate training at St. Philomena's.

1842 January 16, he made his first religious profession as a Redemptorist. He was the first to make profession as a Redemptorist in America.

1844 He became pastor of St. Philomena's and Superior of the community.

1847 He was sent to Baltimore. While there he was appointed Superior of the Redemptorists in America.

1851 He was appointed rector of St. Alphonsus Church, Baltimore, and became confessor to Archbishop Francis Kenrick.

1852 March 28, he was consecrated Bishop of Philadelphia.

1852 He travelled to Europe for the Church's Proclamation of the Immaculate Conception of the Blessed Virgin Mary, his official visit to the Holy Father and a visit to his family in Prachatitz, Bohemia.

1860 January 5, he died of an attack of apoplexy.

1921 John Neumann was declared *Venerable* by Pope Benedict XV in December.

1963 October 13, he was declared *Blessed* by Pope Paul VI.

1977 June 19, he was canonized by Pope Paul VI.

"That Christ be formed in me."

St. John Nepomucene Neumann, C.SS.R.,
Fourth Bishop of Philadelphia